On Course for the Open

A Pictorial Autobiography

With thanks to Bride Hall, Pringle and Wilson for their contribution towards this book

On Course for the Open

A Pictorial Autobiography

Nick Faldo

with Mitchell Platts

Stanley Paul

London Melbourne Auckland Johannesburg

Stanley Paul & Co. Ltd

An imprint of Century Hutchinson Ltd
62-65 Chandos Place, London WC2N 4NW

Century Hutchinson New Zealand Limited
191 Archers Road, PO Box 40-086, Glenfield, Auckland 10
Melbourne, Victoria 3122

Century Hutchinson New Zealand Limited
PO Box 40-086, Glenfield, Auckland 10

Century Hutchinson South Africa (Pty) Ltd
PO Box 337, Bergvlei 2012, South Africa

First published 1987

© Nick Faldo 1987

Set in Linotron Ehrhardt

Design and typesetting by Roger Walker Design Studio

Printed in Great Britain by Scotprint Ltd, Musselburgh, Scotland
Bound by WBC Bookbinders Ltd, Maesteg, Glamorgan

ISBN 0 09 173544 0

PHOTOGRAPHIC ACKNOWLEDGEMENTS

For permission to reproduce copyright material, the
publishers would particularly like to thank Phil Sheldon,
who supplied the majority of the photographs. Thanks also
to Lawrence Levy/Yours in Sport, Peter Dazeley,
Matthew Harris, All-Sport, Alan Raymond, Nic Cooper
and Walt Disney Corporation

Contents

Still my favourite picture of Gill and I – taken by a non-professional
photographer, my cousin Dave Smalley!

Family, friends and fans –
thank you for your love, support and encouragement

Introduction

The photograph on the opposite page shows Tony Jacklin, Sandy Lyle and myself standing together with an elegant golden chalice that is better known as the Ryder Cup. It was taken in 1985 at The Belfry following Europe's historic victory over the United States in the biennial match. Tony, the European captain, had, of course, reached an individual Everest in 1969 when he won the Open Championship. Sandy became the first Briton to follow in the footsteps of Jacklin when he won the Open at Royal St George's in 1985. So at the time that our photograph was taken it showed two Open champions and one golfer still reaching out for the most prestigious prize in the game. Me.

The value of that photograph must have risen sometime after five o'clock on Sunday 19 July! I holed a putt on the last green at Muirfield then waited in the wings as my one remaining rival, Paul Azinger, completed his round. I waited ten, fifteen maybe twenty minutes, in one of the Royal and Ancient offices. It seemed more like a lifetime. Then I knew, along with the thousands surrounding the 18th green and the millions watching on television, that the Open Championship was mine. I had followed Tony and Sandy, and all the other greats, like Taylor and Vardon, Jones and Hagen, Cotton and Thomson, Palmer and Player, Nicklaus and Trevino, Ballesteros and Watson, in reaching the summit of the sport.

Childhood
1957–71

My parents always encouraged me to participate in various sports and I responded by winning awards which I know they cherished as much as me. This one is for all-round achievement on the sporting front. Mr Harvey, my first games teacher, wrote in my school report: 'Nick's future will be in sport. He sets his standards high and dedication will be the key to his success.' I was also fortunate to be fairly strong even in those formative years. I remember that at the age of ten I became the youngest person in the school to get a gold medal for life-saving. I loved swimming and I was the Herts Under-11 freestyle and breaststroke champions over 110 yards

Coincidentally my finest hour came only twenty-four hours after my thirtieth birthday. I was born Nicholas Alexander Faldo on Thursday 18 July 1957, at three o'clock in the afternoon. My mother is seen here holding me when I was only a few days old. Home was a two-bedroom council house at 285, Knella Road, in Welwyn Garden City. My mother, Joyce, was also born in Knella Road.

My father, George, who came from the East End of London, worked in the financial planning department at ICI Plastics. Mum worked as a cutter and pattern drafter for Cresta Silks. She later wanted me to become an actor, and tried to heighten my interest in music. Mum also thought I had smashing legs (!) so she took me to fashion shows at Harrods! In the end she graciously accepted defeat. She acknowledged I was interested only in one thing – sport

My parents always wanted the best for me. They were not wealthy, by any means, although my father had traced back the family tree to discover that the Faldos had come over from Italy during the 17th century. He also claims that four centuries earlier there was a knight of some rank called Sir William Faldo and that somewhere down the line somebody must have lost the family fortune! Anyway it cost my father half a week's wages to commission this portrait. It cost two guineas for the sitting alone, although the woman who took the photograph was better known for snapping Royalty! She also had one other dubious claim to fame...she came from Welwyn Garden City!

This is a real knock-out! I scooted-off one day, with Mum's knitted crash helmet as protection, only to collide with a lamp-post. I'm told that I was unconscious for around one minute. I was three years old at the time and I don't think my mother ever felt really sure about me again unless she had me safely in her sights

My mum loved this ladder...
because it kept me quiet for hours! I suppose I could have been practising for the life of a burglar

My first swing! You should take note of how I take my stance. Very Arnold Palmer!

I was four or five years old when I got my first bat and ball. We had a good sized garden at 285 Knella Road, and I spent many happy hours there. In fact I had gone to nursery school at the age of three and then, two years later, to Thumbswood, the local primary school. At the age of seven I moved on to another school, Blackthorn, where my sporting life centred on throwing a cricket ball! I was pretty big in those days – certainly for my age – and I could heave the old cricket ball a good bit further than anybody else. I must admit that it was important to me to win. Then again you have to hate losing, however well you may accept it, if you want to climb to the top in any profession

13

We had two cats when I was young but my favourite was Sam. He would always be with me when I went to sleep, and he was so attached to me that when I sat down for my tea he would perch on a wooden stool nearby

It looks as if this is me doing my 'Born Free' bit outside the King George V Playing Fields in Welwyn Garden City where we had taken the cats for a show. They came second!

I started my soccer career – in my Stanley Matthews football boots! – at left-back, but I later reverted to being goalie... until one unfortunate day. We had a match against another school and I borrowed Mum's best leather gloves. When I got home she asked me where they were. I had left them at the other school. We never got them back... and from that day on I was made to play centre-forward. I don't think I ever gave up football – it gave me up!

With those chubby chops it looks as if I was better fed than the pigeons!

I have come to find fishing a great way to relax. This is probably my first catch – hauled in from Deal Pier during Whitsun, 1969. These three wouldn't feed *me*, let alone the 5000!

A white Christmas in judo suits. I tackle Dad with Grandad (centre) studiously watching as Uncle Charlie guards the brandy(!) and Auntie Glad looks on. I'm just about to give Dad my dreaded Kwang-Fu throw

Another sporting Christmas present! The name Varsity on the rugby ball might have been a subtle hint from Mum and Dad, hoping for great academic things to come. In fact I did manage to pass my exams, despite the sporting distractions, so that I moved on to Sir Frederic Osborn Comprehensive School. The day before I was due to start my first term we moved into a new house at 11, Redwoods, in Welwyn Garden City. It cost my father £5200

I would like to think that I'm rowing the Atlantic alone. In fact I'm on a couple of laps round the Serpentine before going off for tea with Mum and Dad to Harrods – or was it Lyons Corner House!

15

With Dad in our best whistles (my first) off to see Nan. A bit smooth, don't you think, with the white handkerchief in the top pocket?

Camping at Mont St Michel in northern France with Mum giving me the posture instructions – chin-up, chest-out, stomach-in. I loved our family holidays. My Dad bought an Austin A40 and, although we often went to Sheringham, in Norfolk, we also went on several camping trips to France which included touring the Loire area

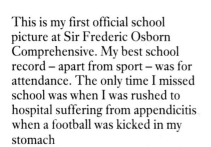

This is my first official school picture at Sir Frederic Osborn Comprehensive. My best school record – apart from sport – was for attendance. The only time I missed school was when I was rushed to hospital suffering from appendicitis when a football was kicked in my stomach

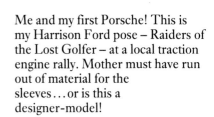

Me and my first Porsche! This is my Harrison Ford pose – Raiders of the Lost Golfer – at a local traction engine rally. Mother must have run out of material for the sleeves...or is this a designer-model!

Pipped at the post by Seb Coe! Well, that is how I like to look at the end of this cross-country race. I recall that I had not learnt the art of pacing myself at that time. In the trials later that year I was expected to qualify with relative ease but I missed out. The trouble was that the day before I had pushed myself too hard in practice. I took all the steam out of myself and, come the day of the real race, I was shattered. I was so stiff I could hardly move

Preparing for our first outside expedition. My mate, Steve Ellis, and I were virtually inseparable all the time at Sir Fred's. He went off to become a plumber and I went to the practice ground

My father and I enjoyed some marvellous times together. We built this canoe from a kit in the spare bedroom. But we did the ultimate – we had failed to think about getting it out! In the end we passed it through the window. My maiden voyage was an unmitigated disaster. I was attacked by a swan and I capsized the canoe! That was the end of the canoe

I loved cycling. This is me, aged fourteen, at the Hemel Hempstead Road Trials in August, 1971. I won a £6 voucher for riding ten miles in the most improved time – 1 minute 42 seconds quicker than my first effort one month earlier. I put a great deal of effort into that sport, out of school time, and I graduated to grade four. One standard higher and I might have attracted the attention of the instructors and been on the road to becoming a Sean Kelly or a Stephen Roche. The trouble was that my sports buds had been whetted earlier that year by another pastime – golf

Amateur Days
1971–5

Ian Connelly, my coach for the first ten years of my career, joined Welwyn Garden City in 1966. He fired my ambition by constantly talking about the great championships of the game. He always drummed into me how good I would become. He taught me all the fundamentals, and I listened and learned, and he told me that only determination and dedication would take me to the top. I was determined and dedicated enough. In the winter I would even sweep the snow off the practice ground so that I could keep hitting balls no matter how cold it was. During the time that we worked together, Ian was my biggest fan and my biggest critic

How I came to look at the television that Easter Sunday I will never know. But it transformed my life. You see, sitting in front of the TV had no appeal to a sports fanatic. I wanted to be running across the field or swimming, hammering the ball into the back of the net or slamming a six, and so television simply was not part of my life. My parents, however, had bought a new colour television. It caught my attention that day and I shall never forget the beautiful picture I saw. It was of Jack Nicklaus striking a ball with the background of lovely green trees. This, then, was Augusta, home of the US Masters, and, more importantly, I was watching the greatest golfer in the history of the game. I was transfixed by what I saw. There is a time in each one of our lives when somebody or something causes a spectacular change in your outlook. I had played virtually every sport one does as a youngster except for golf. I had heroes, like every other sporting schoolboy, but incredibly, or so it seems now, I did not know the name of Jack Nicklaus. I did not even know the name of Tony Jacklin, coincidentally an assistant at one time at Potters Bar, a club not too many miles from Welwyn Garden City, who was to inject life into the British golf scene. It was Jacklin's success in the Open Championship in 1969 – the first by a British player since Max Faulkner in 1951 – which started the big Golf Rush in our country. I vowed to join it that Easter, and by the summer of 1971 I knew that as far as the future was concerned there would be only one sport for me. Golf

I was comfortable in sand even at that age! Sixteen years later, at Muirfield, I walked off the golf course knowing that hours of dedicated practice – and that is what it takes – in the bunkers around the world contributed to my victory in the Open Championship

The Open Championship, the most glorious yet the most elusive prize in golf, was already THE ambition. I had been converted and I could think of nothing else but golf. I redesigned the front of my bike, using a chunk of wood, so that I could strap the bag on and ride the two miles to Welwyn Garden City Golf Club.

I received my first lessons there from Chris Arnold, the assistant. My mother took me along to the club, and he suggested that I should have six lessons so as to determine whether or not I was really interested. It was sound advice but I was already hooked. It was hard on my parents because golf is not an inexpensive sport. The lessons with Chris cost 50p a time. I needed shoes, and also a glove as my hands, sore and bleeding, required protection because of the time I spent on the practice ground.

In fact my grandfather had given me a hickory two-iron when I was eight years old. But I had used it to sweep a clearing in the woods so that my mates and I could build a camp! How I wished for that club now. But Graham Thomas, my deputy headmaster when I was at Blackthorn Primary School, heard of my interest in golf. He rummaged through his garage where he discovered a seven and an eight iron. They were my first clubs.

It was on my fourteenth birthday that I received my first half-set as a present from my parents. They were 'St Andrews' junior clubs and my parents purchased them from Ian Connelly, the professional at Welwyn Garden City, for £35. I had applied for membership and, with the clubs strapped to my bike, I cycled to the club for my first real game.

I can still remember how that first time I missed out the opening hole. I felt I should not be there so I nipped round to the second green.

By the time I had finished the round I was ready for something to eat. I always took with me a tupperware lunch box with my favourite cheddar cheese and salad cream sandwiches and, of course, the inevitable Penguin chocolate biscuit! I sat down and I looked at my first card. I had hit the ball 78 times. I had lost three balls. I had missed out the first hole. And I hadn't counted all the putts! I declared it a practice round and I decided then and there that I would take every round of golf I played seriously from that moment on.

It was treacherous cycling home through the woods, down a one-in-one muddy hill, and I came off my bike on several occasions, finishing head-first in the bushes. But I was a fanatic about the game now and nothing could put me off. I think my parents knew that, which is why they took this picture of me in our back garden at Redwoods. Maybe I *would* have liked a new pair of slippers that Christmas!

My parents, however, were fantastic. I cannot thank them enough. My father, of course, was busy at work during the day but my mother would drive me to this and that event as my competitive instincts got stronger and stronger. My first win was as a junior at John O'Gaunt Golf Club. I shot rounds of 71 and 77, off a handicap of seven, and I won the first Cup of my golf career. It is only five inches high but to this day it remains one of my most treasured possessions

21

There were times, however, when I was compelled to take a break from the fairways. In the Easter of 1972, exactly one year after I had fallen head over heels in love with golf, I was chosen to go on a Duke of Edinburgh Outward Bound course. I spent one month at Ullswater, in the Lake District, and the second half of the stay was a most unpleasant experience. It snowed, and freezing rain made life even more uncomfortable, but on the three days' 'unescorted' survival examination I came to terms with the fact that you get from this life what you are prepared to put into it. That one month at Ullswater sharpened my ambition. And whilst the governor there would say to our group, 'This is the crowd I would like to get to the barbers!' the joke is we were voted the best patrol

I had played for Hertfordshire's senior county team, against some of the best amateurs from other counties, but I had never been prouder than that day in 1974 when I was selected for England to play against Scotland in the British Boys' Championship at Hoylake. I lost both my matches but I felt at the time that it was a cornerstone in my career. For it was also the first time that I met Gerald Micklem, who is one of the finest and most respected administrators in the game. Mr Micklem's interest in me was to be fanned, ironically, more by my indifferent play that week. He was, to be honest, not that impressed. But he was to be impressed by the progress that I was to make that winter. Mr Micklem was probably also not too impressed with my hair at Hoylake, although if you think mine is bad then take a look at young Ken Brown (second from the right in the front row). Sandy Lyle (centre, front row) looks as if he's just done two years square-bashing!

England Boys' (left to right) – back row: Andrew Jackson, Paul Downes, Malcolm Latham, Nick Faldo, Peter Davies, Trevor Patmore, Jeff Hall. Front row: Tony Higgins, Paul Hoad, Sandy Lyle, Ken Brown, Brian Whitby

23

During the winter of 1974-5 I worked harder than ever on my game. Then on 3 April I won the Royston Boys' Championship with a score of 140, and twelve days later I captured the Hertfordshire Junior County Championship with a total of 144 at Verulam GC, St Albans. It was the start of a phenomenal year. Mr Micklem saw me play in the West of England Championship at Taunton, in Devon, and I am reliably informed that he could scarcely believe the progress that I had made during that winter. I became on 15 June, at the age of seventeen, the youngest winner of The Berkshire Trophy, with a 72-

holes score of 281, and I was subsequently awarded the Scrutton Jug, given to the player with the lowest aggregate in the Brabazon Trophy, in which I had finished joint seventh with a score of 306, and The Berkshire Trophy. Then, after winning the Hertfordshire County Championship at Ashridge, I became the youngest-ever winner of the English Amateur Championship. I was eight days beyond my eighteenth birthday when I defeated David Eccleston 6 and 4 in the 36-holes final at Royal Lytham and St Anne's. It was the moment that I suddenly realized that something was happening in

the life of Nick Faldo. Ian Erskine, then the secretary of the English Golf Union, declared at the presentation: 'And the champion golfer of England is...Nick Faldo!'

Then came the Youths' International at Pannal, Harrogate, on 5 August in which I won my singles. The team (left to right) was – back row: Peter Deeble, Steve Martin, Peter Wilson, Nigel Burch, Gary Harvey, Sandy Stephen. Front row: Mark James, Martin Poxon, John Watts, Nick Faldo (note the white shoes!), Sandy Lyle

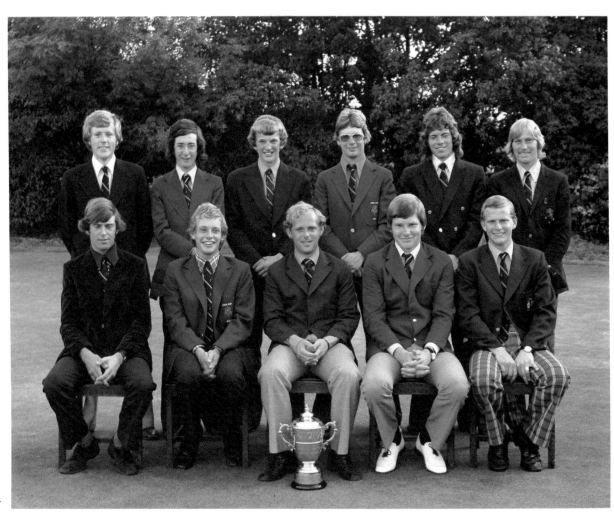

It was a marvellous week for me at Pannal. I beat Massimo Mannelli, of Italy, in the match between Great Britain and Ireland and the Continent of Europe; then on 9 August I won the British Youths' Championship with rounds of 65,74,70 and 69.

That led to my first flight. We were flown to Dublin for The Home Internationals at Portmarnock. I recall that we arrived so early that Chris Mitchell, one of our players, was chosen to climb through a toilet window – he was the skinniest among us and the window only measured about 20 inches by 10 inches – to open a door as the club was still locked. He made it through the window but once on the inside he slipped and…flushed the loo! I managed to win 4½ points out of 6 so it was not too bad considering the importance of the Internationals.

The England team (left to right) was – back row: Peter Deeble,Chris Mitchell, Martin Poxon, Mike Kelly, Sandy Lyle, Richard Eyles, Rodney James. Front row: Mark James, Nick Faldo, Michael Lunt, Geoffrey Marks, Peter Hedges

25

It was back to Welwyn Garden City on 21 September where I won the club championship by defeating D.C. Allen 7 and 5 in the final. Then, after winning the County Champions' Tournament for the President's Bowl at Kedleston Park, Derby, later that month, it was back to Welwyn Garden City for a special presentation. Clive Harkett, who did so much to inspire confidence in me when I was at W.G.C. as a junior, presented me with the W.G.C. Championship Trophy at a celebration dinner for me on 21 December 1975. I had only shortly before returned from South Africa where I won the South African Golf Union Special Stroke Play Championship at Mowbray, Cape Town, and played for Great Britain in the British Commonwealth Trophy Tournament at Royal Durban.

The trophies on display that night at Welwyn Garden City (Clive is presenting me with the Club Championship Trophy) were (left to right): The Scrutton Jug, Hertfordshire County Championship, the English Amateur Open Stroke Play Championship, Hertfordshire Junior County Championship, The Berkshire Trophy, British Youths' Championship, County Champions' Tournament for the President's Bowl

Following my astonishing results in 1975, I took a golf scholarship at the University of Houston. I initially went there with Sandy Lyle and Martin Poxon. I won a freshman's tournament and I played in three matches for the University. But I decided to return home. I felt I was spending too much time in the classroom and not enough time on the practice range. So back I came on 14 March 1976. I mapped out another year on the amateur circuit. My first trip was to Scotland for the King George IV Trophy at Craigmillar Park. It was to be my last as an amateur. I won and I decided, returning home, that I wanted to become a professional. My brown bag had nothing on it but the name of Nick Faldo. Soon I would have a tournament bag with my professional attachments emblazoned on it

Professional Breakthrough
1976–9

In action in my early professional days

The move from amateur to professional is not an easy one. It is suddenly a different game out there. You are playing for your living. You know when you hit that first ball in a professional tournament that from that moment on it is a case of grinding it out if you want to fulfill all your dreams. I hit my first shot as a professional in the French Open at Le Touquet on 6 May 1976. My first advice as a professional came from Ben Crenshaw. His message to me at the French Open was: 'Go out and win the French title and set your sights no lower.' I didn't win but I finished a creditable joint 38th. I had some good results in that first season which included finishing joint 10th in the German Open at Frankfurt. I was not happy with the way the season ended. I missed the halfway cut in the Carrolls Irish Open – coincidentally won by Crenshaw! – then failed to pre-qualify for the Sun Alliance Match Play championship and the Benson and Hedges International. But while it showed me the pitfalls of the professional game it also taught me not to get despondent. You cannot afford to lose heart in this game. I had finished 58th in the Order of Merit – worth prize money of £2112! – and I regarded it as a solid if not spectacular start. But I was on my way.

My first success came in the Skol Lager Individual event on the King's Course at Gleneagles Hotel. I had begun 1977 by missing the halfway cut in the Portuguese Open. Two weeks later I was joint 3rd in the Madrid Open at Club de Campo. I had made an impact. I was joint 6th a few weeks later in the Penfold PGA Championship at Royal St George's. It was to be the start of a long and lasting love affair not only with that Championship but also with links golf. Then at Moor Park, a course I knew well from my amateur days, I won my

way into a play-off with Seve Ballesteros following rounds of 68, 67, 73 and 68 in the Uniroyal International Championship. Seve won at the first extra hole but I knew now that it was only a matter of time. I finished 3rd three weeks later in the German Open then, after another play-off, I took the Skol title by defeating Craig Defoy and Chris Witcher at the first extra hole. I took Mum and Dad out for dinner at the Gleneagles Hotel to celebrate

Ian Connelly had said at the start of 1977, 'Let's make the Ryder Cup team.' I agreed it was something to go for but it seemed a distant dream. Yet later that year at Royal Lytham and St Anne's I enjoyed the most memorable week of my life. Tom Watson had, of course, won the Open Championship at Turnberry that summer following his amazing duel with Jack Nicklaus. I had finished joint 62nd which was disappointing because in my first Open at Royal Birkdale the previous year I had filled joint 28th place. The Ryder Cup, however, more than compensated for my

backward step at the Open. I was the youngest ever to play in the biennial match against the United States and it was a thrill, too, for my caddie, John Moorhouse. We had played as juniors at Welwyn Garden City, and when I turned professional his father suggested that John should work for me. We were a good partnership through to 1979. He was a very good caddie and he later worked for Mark James with whom he stayed until he 'retired' from golf in 1985

The Ryder Cup was the most nerve-racking experience of my life. By the time I came to meet Tom Watson, who was obviously the biggest scalp on offer that week, I was feeling a little easier because I had won my foursomes and fourballs in company with Peter Oosterhuis. Our victories included Jack Nicklaus and Ray Floyd! But with Watson it was almost as if the draw had been rigged which, of course, it hadn't. It was the ultimate draw for me. He was the Open champion and I was on my way up. It seemed to me that it was the match that everybody had wanted

I served my apprenticeship that Ryder Cup alongside Peter Oosterhuis. I think Brian Hugget, the captain, might have initially paired us together because Peter is 6ft 5ins and I'm 6ft 3ins. Brian was very secretive in his selections, but as Peter and I practised together, and appeared to be dovetailing quite nicely, I thought I might just start the match. We went out against Lou Graham and Ray Floyd and won 2 and 1. I had the daunting task of teeing-off at the first hole – a par three – and before moving to the tee I hit twenty extra five irons and twenty extra four irons on the practice ground. My first Ryder Cup shot landed safely on the green, but Peter left me with a teasing three-foot putt. I missed. I hadn't hit a bad putt but I had missed. I knew it wasn't nerves but it still hurt. Even so we went on to win – the only British winners in that first session – and we did so again in the fourballs against Jack Nicklaus and Ray Floyd. I had never met Jack before. For some reason I was in the mood that day just to get on the tee and give it a rip. I recall that Jack, arms folded, kept scowling at me as I outdrove him. I just kept looking forward and walking forward. Oosty was great. He encouraged me all the way and we finally won 2 and 1

Then came the match against Tom Watson – and a win for me on the final green! It was the icing on the cake for me, and I was whisked away for my first radio interview with Desmond Lynam, who was also a bit of a 'rookie' then. It was also the first time that I really came in contact with enthusiastic autograph hunters

I arrived at my first World Match Play Championship – then sponsored by Colgate – having won a 54-hole limited field tournament in Belgium for the Laurent Perrier Trophy. My Mum and Dad wanted this picture taken because they both had new 'specs'. 'All the better for watching you play golf in, Nick,' they said, but I'm not sure if they kept them on. I was beaten 4 and 2 in the first round by Seve Ballesteros! The World Match Play Championship is a great spectacle and it is one of my ambitions to become the first British player to win it

I had finished 8th in the Order of
Merit in 1977, but the next season
did not start as well as I would have
liked. I failed to make the top ten in
four continental tournaments. But I
returned home and finished 2nd in
the Martini International – edged
out again by that man Seve. But I
knew that my swing was in good
shape at that time, my tempo and
rhythm were great, and at the
Colgate PGA Championship at
Royal Birkdale on 29 May 1978 I
swung my way to a golden victory

I had birdied three of the last four holes in the third round so I went into the final day with a four-shot lead over Peter Townsend and Howard Clark with Dale Hayes, of South Africa, one shot further adrift. But I dropped a shot at the 1st and 3rd holes and I was in danger of doing so again at the 4th until I reached for my trusty Ray Cook mallet putter and rolled the ball home from twelve feet to salvage a morale-boosting par. I had bought the putter secondhand in the pro shop at Welwyn Garden City, and it proved a faithful friend to me. I've kept every putter that I've won tournaments with

My final round of 69 had given me a ten under par winning aggregate of 278. I finished seven shots ahead of my former Herts Colts team-mate Ken Brown, while Howard Clark took third place on 286. I think Ken has had an acute attack of hay fever here!

At the prize-giving, where David
Foster of Colgate presented me
with the trophy, I remarked to the
club captain that perhaps the Royal
Birkdale Club would like to offer
the first three junior membership
because we were all so young! Ken
Brown and I had, of course, played
many matches together so it was
great to finish 1–2. We were
virtually unbeatable for Herts Colts
as Ken, then one of the quickest
players, had this happy knack of
being able to chip-in at least three
times a round

In fact Ken Brown had his turn later in the year when he won the Carrolls Irish Open at Portmarnock. This picture of Seve and I was taken at the course that week. Seve had won three times already that season in Europe and he was to make it four in the Swiss Open the following week. He had a massive, high swing in those days and he took an almighty cut at the ball. But we all knew from the start that there was something magical about him

It was a bitter-sweet summer for me. In the Open Championship at St Andrews I played well but I eventually finished joint 7th behind Jack Nicklaus. When I look back it was, of course, part of the learning process leading to 1987 and all that. The Open Championship had become my target and everything that I did in golf was aimed at preparing myself for that one big day when it eventually came.

There were, of course, other moments to savour. I had my first hole-in-one at the third hole at Welwyn Garden City in 1973 and I've still got the ball. I had my second in the German Open in 1978 and later that year I did it again at the 191-yards 17th hole in the third round of the European Open at Walton Heath. I achieved all three aces – the only ones of my life so far – with a six iron.

The one in Germany still rankles with me. There was a £17,000 Mercedes 450 SL for the first professional to hole in one, but I made my ace on the Pro-Am day which did not count. That evening I had dinner with Tony Jacklin. He said he would make an ace some-time during the event to make me feel really mad. I said I fancied my chances of doing it again. So we had a £1000 side bet so that if either one of us pulled it off we would give the other the £1000 as 'compensation'. In the first round I came within half an inch of doing it. In the third round Tony did it at the 182-yards 15th on the Cologne-Refrath course with...a six iron! I suppose it is the easiest 'grand' I've ever earned!

I played on the United States Tour for the first time in 1979; I received an invitation to the Greater Greensboro Open, where I finished 44th, before travelling south to Augusta for my first US Masters. In fact I had called in to Augusta on the way to Greensboro because I couldn't wait to take my first look at this historic course. I played a couple of practice rounds and it was simply fantastic. Augusta is so beautifully manicured and those rolling fairways, with not a divot in sight, are absolutely magnificent. What they have never done at Augusta is take the driver out of the bag, whereas at some of the other major championships the courses are now set-up so that you have to play safe with a one iron or a three wood. I finished 40th at my first Masters but Joe – it was compulsory to take a local caddie at that time – was not too clever. They always said that the local caddies were wonderful. It's a joke. He didn't

know a thing. He was only useful
for telling me the way to the next
tee. He clubbed me so badly that on
the first day I hit a shot that went
sailing over the back of the green! It
hit this chap smack on the forehead.
Thankfully he was OK and the ball
bounced back to eight feet from the
hole, but I hadn't the heart to hole it!

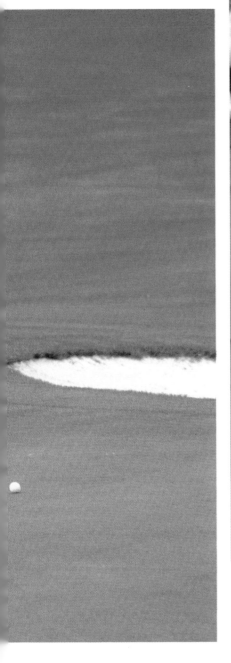

Giving it a blast at Augusta. It has to
be my ambition now to win another
major championship very quickly
and the US Masters would do very
nicely, thank-you very much

41

I did not have a great year in Europe in 1979 – slipping from 3rd in the Order of Merit the previous year to 21st – and I was less than satisfied with my showing in the Open Championship at Royal Lytham and St Anne's as I finished joint 19th. But there had been much for Europe to celebrate as Seve Ballesteros had won the Open. Moreover the growing strength of the continental golfers had been noted by Jack Nicklaus and it was following a conversation that he had with Lord Derby, the President of the PGA, that it was agreed that a European team should now contest the Ryder Cup against the Americans. So our team at The Greenbrier, West Virginia, was (left to right) – back row: Mark James, Sandy Lyle, Nick Faldo, Peter Oosterhuis, Antonio Garrido, Bernard Gallacher. Front row: Des Smyth, Ken Brown, Tony Jacklin, John Jacobs (captain), Severiano Ballesteros, Brian Barnes, Michael King

Peter Oosterhuis and I, of course, stayed as partners. We lost to Andy Bean and Lee Elder in the opening fourballs, but we beat Mark Hayes and Elder in the next series of fourballs having overcome Andy Bean and Tom Kite in the foursomes. Although we lost 17–11 there were signs at that match that the Americans could be beaten. John Jacobs, too, was a pretty good captain. He doesn't have Tony Jacklin's charisma but we had a lot of faith in him and the players voted him back for 1981. Lord Derby agreed

I think that Ryder Cup is famous for
the fact that nobody came to watch.
Seve, seen here putting, had an
unhappy debut winning only 1 point
out of 5 but I managed to get 3
points out of 4. I kept my 100 per
cent individual record intact by
44 beating Lee Elder 3 and 2

American Education
1980–2

I got my first in-depth view of the US Tour during 1981, when I played in eleven tournaments in all. This is me, on cloud nine at the Hawaiian Open, holing from 15 feet for a two at the 17th hole on the way to completing a second round of 62. I was the halfway leader. Then the next day I played with Hale Irwin; he shot 62, and I handed in a 72 and finished joint 40th!

I have to admit that 1979 was a disappointing year in my life. I had expected better things, following my victory the previous year in the PGA Championship, but it was not to be. Yet after all the anguish and apprehension in Europe it took me only one tournament in South Africa to find winning form again. I won the ICL International at Kensington, on the outskirts of Johannesburg, with rounds of 68, 66, 69 and 65. It was not only an extremely satisfying success – my first professional win abroad – but it also put me in the right frame of mind for 1980. I had top ten finishes in three of my first five events that year and then it was back to being a champion again

I have gone back to the Bullseye Blade – the putter I first used when I turned pro – and it worked a treat for me at Royal St George's, Sandwich, as I holed putt after putt on my way to victory in the Sun Alliance PGA Championship. I won that Championship by practising hundreds and hundreds of long irons. There are no fewer than eight holes at Sandwich where you are going into the greens with a long iron. In fact I very much enjoy the course when it is green, but when it gets burnt it is almost too difficult

Another win on a links course had convinced me that I was ready for the Open Championship at Muirfield. I certainly practised in the right company as Andy North and I took on Jack Nicklaus and Tom Watson. It was really hot, and it was taking time to get round, so at the 3rd Andy bought a round of ice creams. Jack did the same at the 6th and I weighed-in at the 9th. Then at the 15th Andy said to Tom: 'Isn't it your turn to get the ice creams in?' Tom said he didn't want one, but Andy marched over to his bag and 'borrowed' Tom's wallet. The day before Andy had lost £30 to Tom in a practice match. Now he stood by the ice cream van offering every Tom, Dick and Harry the chance to have an ice cream on Tom until he had spent £30. Then he gave Tom his wallet back. It was a good day for me because I took a tenner off Jack. Foolishly I spent it instead of getting him to sign it for posterity. I came joint 12th behind Watson, who had the last laugh!

49

My only other win that season was in the *Golf World* Long Driving contest! I made up a graphite-shafted driver, with the assistance of Barry Willett, a master at the craft of club making, and with it I could launch a ball unbelievable distances. In the final I pipped Bernhard Langer by one yard

My first sojourn in the States meant tackling the European tour in a different way. I missed the initial continental segment and started at the Martini International. It was business as usual the next week (!) as I won the PGA Championship for a third time in four years. My bunker play that week was excellent

I have always placed enormous
importance on practising the short
game, and as I put together rounds
of 68, 70, 67 and 69 to win with an
aggregate of 274 I was proud of the
way I played some of the chip shots

My swing was also in good shape
but I was not so happy with what
happened after I had put in my card
for the last round. Greg Norman,
Ken Brown and myself were all
fined for slow play. It wasn't the £50
they slapped on us but the principle
of it. There was no warning

53

Andy Prodger, whom I had taken on after John Moorhouse left, enjoyed the week. He has always been a very good caddie, but he is a quiet old soul and we were to break up at the Lancome Trophy in 1982 mostly through lack of communication. But he was back with me at the Open Championship in 1987 – and we both enjoyed that!

It really is great to see your name up there at the end of the tournament. Let's face it, the name of the game is winning

	DARD	SUN ALLIANCE PGA CHAMPIONSHIP		
	SCORE			
	274			
	278			
	278			
	281			
		SCORE AFTER 17	**PLAYER**	**SCORE FOR ROUND**
E			DAVIS	75
A			COLES	67
HIP			BEMBRIDGE	71
		66	NORMAN	72
R		65	BROWN	70
		65	FALDO	69

55

My eyes were now trained once more, of course, on the Open Championship, but a first round of 77 at Royal St George's was hardly the springboard to success. I followed-up with scores of 68, 69, and 73 for joint 11th place, but the American Bill Rogers had set sail for home never to be caught by anyone.

I didn't win again in 1981 but I managed to finish 2nd in the Order of Merit courtesy of a succession of consistent performances which included finishing 2nd to Sandy Lyle in the Lawrence Batley International and 2nd to Sam Torrance in the Carrolls Irish Open.

The Ryder Cup, too, was back in Britain – at Walton Heath – and I felt we had a chance until I saw their team. This was their World War III outfit with Crenshaw, Floyd, Kite, Miller, the unbeatable Larry Nelson, Nicklaus, Open champion Rogers, Trevino and Watson among them. They demolished us 18½–9½. We didn't help ourselves, if you take a look at the team picture and spot the missing man. Severiano Ballesteros was left out that year and, even taking into account all the politics behind that decision, it was ludicrous for us to go into battle without him.

Our team (left to right) was – back row: Manuel Pinero, Bernhard Langer, Des Smyth, Eamonn Darcy, Sandy Lyle, Mark James, José-Maria Canizares, Bernard Gallacher. Front row: Howard Clark, Sam Torrance, John Jacobs (captain), Peter Oosterhuis, Nick Faldo

I started out again with Peter Oosterhuis, but it was to be our last Ryder Cup match together. It was a bit awesome because we tackled Jack Nicklaus and Tom Watson, who were both in peak form that week, and we were moderately stuffed 4 and 3. I salvaged something from the week by beating Johnny Miller 2 and 1 in the singles

I had another busy programme in America at the start of 1982, but I returned to Britain for the Martini International in which I finished joint 2nd behind Bernard Gallacher. The weeks were slipping by without a win, but I felt that my efforts in America had helped to prepare me for another Open Championship challenge. I went to Royal Troon full of hope and I played well. Tom Watson, however, played better, winning with an aggregate of 284, but I was joint 4th only two shots behind. I felt that I was making progress. I felt that one day the Open Championship would be mine

I finally won again in the Haig Whisky Tournament Players Championship. I don't think the members at Hollinwell were too pleased with me because the Notts Golf Club, as it is known, is a tough test and I took the title with rounds of 69, 67, 65 and 69. But it was a dry week, with plenty of run on the fairways, although I was under some pressure as I had been told that I would have to win if I wanted to play in the World Match Play Championship later that year.

In fact it turned out to be a World Match Play Championship that I prefer to forget, as I allowed a healthy lead to slip away against Sandy Lyle. I eventually lost 2 and 1 in the first round. I did finish the year 4th in the Order of Merit but I hardly came out firing on all cylinders following the winter recess

Success in Europe
1983–5

Bernhard Langer and I linked together well from the start when Tony Jacklin
decided to pair us for the Ryder Cup match against the Americans at the PGA
National Club in Palm Beach Gardens, Florida, at the end of 1983

There is no doubt that 1983 turned my career around. I captured five tournaments in Europe on the way to topping the Order of Merit for the first time. Yet it started with a run of miserable performances in the United States. I missed the halfway cut in three of my first four tournaments and my best effort did not come until April when I was 6th in the Greater Greensboro Open. Then I moved on to Augusta where I finished joint 20th. The next week I missed the cut at the Sea Pines Heritage Classic – a tournament I was to win twelve months later – and after that it was a phone call halfway through the Byron Nelson Classic which lit the blue touch paper on a new chapter in my career.

The call came from my manager, John Simpson, who said that Greg Norman, the star attraction at the French Open the following week, was going into hospital for a leg operation and would I be prepared to fly over and play. I felt like giving it a go because I was experimenting with a new swing, after working on opening the club more on the takeaway with the American golfer Mark O'Meara, and I reckoned that a run on the European circuit would do the trick.

At the Racing Club de France, on the outskirts of Paris, I tied with David J. Russell and the Spaniard José-Maria Canizares. I made it into the play-off with an eagle at the 18th – hitting a driver then a two iron to 15 feet from where I holed the putt. Russell departed at the first extra hole and Canizares hit his ball into a bush at the third

I went on to the Martini International at Wilmslow where I finished with two 66s to squeeze into another play-off, again with Canizares. This time poor José-Maria missed a tiddler at the third extra hole and I made it two out of two

The second of many victory speeches that year

I equalled Peter Alliss's achievement of three wins in a row on the European circuit by putting together rounds of 67, 68, 68 and 69 for an aggregate of 272 in the Car Care Plan International at Sand Moor, Leeds. My goal on returning to Europe had been to become a multi-winner. I felt that with this win I had achieved it, although I was obviously looking for more that season. Even so I had won £31,954 in twenty-one days, which couldn't be bad at around £40 a stroke

The Open Championship remained the primary target. And, looking back, I could have won that title as well in 1983 at Royal Birkdale. Perhaps I am wondering here how it got away as I momentarily led on the last afternoon. But it is all part of the learning process. When you realize how much pressure there is involved, then I'm glad I had such experiences as 1983 because it helped me to cope when my time came in 1987. When I was an amateur I remember Gerald Micklem telling me that you had to blow six tournaments before you could think of winning one. I think there is some truth in that. At Royal Birkdale it turned for me when I was on the green in two at the long 13th – putting for an eagle from 40 feet – and walked off the green with a five. I struck the first putt four feet past and I missed the return. I at least felt that I had given the first putt a chance

I was exhausted after the Open and I didn't really feel like playing in the Lawrence Batley International at Bingley St Ives, Bradford. But I put on my American outfit – like the check trousers! – and teed it up. I knew I couldn't throw the towel in because of the Order of Merit and after opening rounds of 71 and 69 I produced closing rounds of 64 and 62. I had scored my fourth win of the season on a course which starts and finishes with par threes. Lawrence Batley himself is a golf nut. He loves to have a practice round with you, although his great thing is to listen to a two-hour tape by American golfer Al Geiberger. So I'll let you into a little secret: if you ever see Lawrence on the course, just tell him he's hitting the ball like Al Geiberger. You'll be his friend for life!

I completed my European nap hand with an astonishing win in the Ebel Swiss Open European Masters on the Crans-sur-Sierre course, 5000 feet high in the Swiss Alps. I was eleven strokes behind Sandy Lyle with 22 holes to play and I was still six in arrears with 16 remaining. But I managed to take Sandy to a play-off and he missed a tiddler of a putt at the second extra hole to hand victory to me on a plate. It was a big week for me because it meant that I was number one in the European Order of Merit. I did really well out of that. It opened the

doors to the major championships in the United States and it changed my life financially. All my contracts were up at the end of the year so John Simpson could renegotiate for me. My commercial deals were tripled!

Malcolm Folley, of the *Mail on Sunday*, was their golf correspondent but he also covered the motor racing scene. He fixed up for me to go to Thruxton. Ian Taylor, the instructor there, sent me out for a couple of laps in a saloon car – to check that I knew

which way to go! – and then he put me into this Formula Four. It only has a 1600 cc engine and I thought it would be a doddle. Far from it. The thing really flew along…But I loved it. It was the first time I had put a crash helmet on. I found that rather claustrophobic especially as it rattles away as you speed along, but I managed to zip through some of the bends doing 120 mph. But I've never done it since. I decided to stick to golf – it's a different ball game!

It had also been a great year for my caddie, David McNeilly, although we had to settle for joint 6th place in the Tournament Players Championship at St Mellion, near Plymouth. David joined me at the start of 1982. On the tour we use a pedometer, known as the wheel, for measuring yardages and I recall my first phone call with David. 'Have you got a wheel?' I enquired. 'No,' he said, 'I use public transport!' From that day on, everything that David said was a classic. He used to call me the 'Rain King' and in 1983,

of course, I had backed up his judgement by winning those first three events in wet and windy conditions. I called him the mad Irishman – he always had a few tricks up his sleeve. We had a great time together through the Benson

and Hedges International in 1985, then our relationship began to get strained. There was no reason for it. Like many things it was just time for a change

A nap hand of trophies (left to right): Swiss Open, Car Care International, Lawrence Batley, French Open and Martini International, shot on location(!) in the picturesque Hertfordshire village of Ayot St Lawrence where I lived at the time

We all had much to thank Tony Jacklin for. It was his first term as Ryder Cup captain, and his enthusiasm was fantastic. He was hoarse through shouting his support on the first day. He always seemed to be at the right place at the right time. Tony wanted to be involved all the time, whereas other captains have taken a backseat. He didn't stand any nonsense and he was quite prepared to take full responsibilty. We might have become then and there the first team to triumph in the Ryder Cup on American soil, but we were edged out in the end 14½–13½

It would have been a nice way to end the season, as would have been a victory in the Suntory World Match Play Championship at Wentworth. I beat Graham Marsh in the first round, then Hale Irwin, and here I'm on my way to a 6 and 5 triumph over New Zealand's Bob Charles in the semi-finals. We know Bob as 'Mr Meticulous' – he even has creases in his waterproofs!

He is still a very fine golfer but I think 36 holes at Wentworth three days in succession was too much for him, even though he has kept himself ultra-fit

It was a fairly miserable day, as you can see, but this golfing extravaganza, staged every autumn at leafy Wentworth, always attracts massive galleries

70

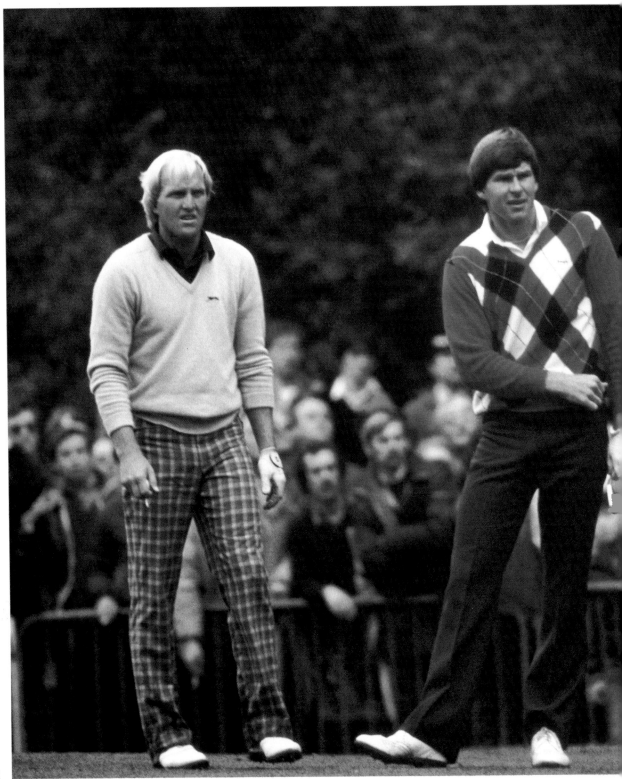

There was certainly a huge crowd there for the final, in which I met the Australian Greg Norman. But I felt that I threw the match away. I was two up in the morning then hit it out of bounds at the 17th. It reduced my advantage at lunch and in the afternoon I had a bad patch. Than at the 11th Greg asked me to leave my ball close to the hole, and he hit a terrible putt. It horseshoed out but hit my ball and tumbled back into the cup. It was a killer blow. The rule allowing you to leave your opponent's ball was changed for the next championship.

Greg, of course, was awesome in 1986 when he topped the American money list and won ten tournaments around the world including the Open Championship at Turnberry. He played for several years on the European circuit, learning the trade like all of us, although I don't think that at that time he had a very good short game. He worked hard on that when he went to live in America and he has been rewarded for his efforts. He's a tough guy to meet. He doesn't give an inch in match-play. You go in against Greg knowing it is going to be a battle

As a result of having such a good year John Simpson (right) was busier than ever on my behalf. We first met in 1977 when I was playing in the PGA Championship at Sandwich. He subsequently joined the International Management Group, and has remained a great friend as well as my manager. It was George Blumberg (left), who sadly died earlier this year, who first helped to negotiate my contract with the International Management Group. He asked Mark McCormack to look after me and 'Uncle George', as we fondly refer to him, was always very good to me

Golf is a game of ups and downs, as I was to find out once again in 1984. At Augusta in the US Masters I really had a great chance to win. I began the last round sharing third place with Ben Crenshaw and David Graham. Sadly, for me, it was to be Ben's day. I was in a good frame of mind. I was ready to go. Yet I made some silly mistakes on the outward half and I couldn't consolidate. It is one of the places where a minor error can prove extremely expensive: hit the ball slightly off line and you will finish in a bunker, as I did at the 10th hole. I finished with a 76 for joint 15th place. I was deflated

I had arrived there with a real make or break attitude. Gill and I had been in America for fourteen weeks and we were exhausted by all the travelling. I told her that she would either be packing on Friday night or on Monday morning because I said that I was going out there to attack: to win the Championship or miss the halfway cut. It would be one or the other. When I tapped the ball in from four inches I knew it was mine. Dave McNeilly and I celebrated.

I had shot rounds of 66, 67, 68 and 69 to win with a fourteen under par aggregate of 270, which equalled the tournament record set by Tom Watson in 1979. Moreover I was the first British golfer to win on American soil since Tony Jacklin in 1972. It was quite a feeling

That evening we celebrated at Evonne's – the nightclub owned by the former Wimbledon champion, Evonne Cawley, and her husband, Roger. They threw a party for us and one of the couples there, friends of ours who owned a chocolate factory nearby, gave us a present. Gill unwrapped it in the morning and it was a chocolate number one.

I moved on the next week to the Sea Pines Heritage Classic at Harbour Town, Hilton Head Island, in South Carolina. I was still thinking of the Masters, of what might have been, and then, one week later, there I was with two putts to win my first tournament on American soil. I had taken a three wood off the last tee, then a six iron for the next shot of 185 yards to the pin. I had a tricky putt from 18 feet, the ball being just off the green, but I gave it a good roll and it finished only four inches from the hole

77

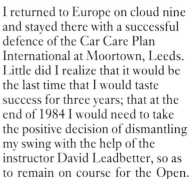

I returned to Europe on cloud nine and stayed there with a successful defence of the Car Care Plan International at Moortown, Leeds. Little did I realize that it would be the last time that I would taste success for three years; that at the end of 1984 I would need to take the positive decision of dismantling my swing with the help of the instructor David Leadbetter, so as to remain on course for the Open.

I was still playing quite nicely and the following week I was 3rd behind Bernhard Langer in the Peugeot French Open at St Cloud, Paris. It was an unusual and memorable week for me because after a first round of 71 I was whisked by a private car to the airport to fly home for a reception given by the Queen and the Duke of Edinburgh on the evening of 14 May 1984 at Buckingham Palace. I chatted in a relaxed manner with Prince Philip for about ten minutes, mostly about sport, and then the Queen spoke to me about my win in the United States. I flew back to Paris the following morning to continue the Championship

I played in my first US Open at
Winged Foot, where I finished joint
55th as Fuzzy Zoeller beat Greg
Norman in a play-off. It remains the
most disappointing event in which
I've played. I expected so much but
the practice facilities were poor and
the transportation and the facilities
for the players and their wives were
non-existent. We stayed in nearby
White Plains and the hotel cost a
small fortune. The fire alarm kept
going off and the floods that week
even sent trees floating down the
road. It was awful. But I had plenty
of time to work on my clubs!

I play a chip shot on the Winged
Foot course, where my scores that
week of 71, 76, 77 and 72 were
nothing to write home about

At the time I felt that at St Andrews I might win the Open Championship. I was still on a high, following my win in America, and, like most golfers, I have a special affinity for the 'old grey toon'. There is also Nick's Bunker at the 13th, and even if it doesn't come into range – it is left off the tee and only 150 yards out – I always take a look at it when I'm there

I went there with high expectations. I knew St Andrews well. I had been fortunate several years earlier when Gerald Micklem had given me three sheets of paper detailing every bunker and hazard, hump and hollow that there was on the Old Course and pointing out the capricious nature of the wind and the pin placements for the Championship. Gerald had been a valued spectator, a fine friend and a person to whom I could also look for guidance. He once saw me throw a club down in disgust in 1975. He came over and told me how he used to do that, then stressed how it never got him

anywhere. I appreciated the way he told me. It wasn't a case of, 'If I ever see you doing that again. . . .' He spoke good sense and I always listened. He is regarded as one of the game's foremost administrators and during his own playing days he was a leading amateur golfer. In the photograph he is pictured centre, with (left to right): Tony Gray, George O'Grady, professional Ken Bousfield, and John Paramor.

Gerald is also quite emotional, as I found out after I won the Open in 1987. I met him at Sunningdale the next day and there were tears in his eyes as he congratulated me. It was such an emotive moment that I could hardly speak myself.

With the assistance of his notes I moved into a challenging position with opening rounds of 69 and 68 – matching those of the eventual winner, Seve Ballesteros – but I blew my chance on the outward half in the third round. I struggled to the turn in 40 and I had to play well coming home into the wind to keep my score to a 76

81

I came back on the last day with a 69 but it was too late. I finished joint 6th, some six shots behind Seve. David Leadbetter, who would later rebuild my swing into an Open Championship-winning one, would cringe at this. And so do I now. The right arm is going into the right pocket! In truth I was really beginning to struggle although I did not realize then what I would have to go through to get back in the groove

I actually played quite well in the US PGA Championship at Shoal Creek that year, and after a first round of 69 I was in the hunt. In fact I was still very much in the picture as I drove off from the 18th in the second round. The trouble was I hit the ball into the rough, hacked out, then put a seven iron into the water. A penalty drop, a chip and three putts later and I had an eight on my card. It was the third time in four major championships that I felt I had allowed a chance of glory to slip from my grasp. I was becoming frustrated. Lee Trevino, however, had a marvellous week as he captured the title by holding off Gary Player in a battle of the 'over forties'. I first met Lee at the Open Championship at Carnoustie in 1975 when his caddie, Willie Aitchison, promised me that I could play a practice round with Lee if I managed to qualify for the Championship. I failed by two shots

I actually made a birdie from out of this bush. I had to! It was my first stint as a captain because I was in charge of the England team in the Hennessy Cognac Cup at Ferndown, Dorset. It was a nice, relaxed week, and we won! So in one respect I did get my hands on another trophy although this was pure team work, with (left to right) Brian Waites, Yours Truly, Howard Clark and Mark James forming the winning team

85

I was back at the Suntory World Match Play Championship, but I wasn't at my best. I lost 4 and 3 to Seve in the second round and he genuinely said: 'I know you can play better than that.' I ended the year back at the Million Dollar Challenge at Sun City, Bophuthatswana, South Africa, and for the second successive time I was runner-up to Seve Ballesteros. More importantly I met David Leadbetter, who would eventually change my career

I began 1985 with a certain amount of apprehension. I had spoken to David Leadbetter at Sun City, and he had certainly provided me with food for thought. I started another year in America but I was far from happy with my game. Even so I was unfortunate not to make the leading twenty-four in the US Masters – I missed by one shot – who automatically claim places for the following year.

You don't want to be in bunkers anywhere in the world but at least the sand at Augusta is excellent from which to play out. There is a bigger hazard at the 16th – water – and this is unquestionably one of the finest holes in the world

I moved on to Hilton Head Island to defend the Sea Pines Heritage Classic. The tradition there is for the champion to hit the ball, teed-up on sand, with an old-fashioned 46-inch shafted club into the water simultaneously to two 'yeomans' firing a cannon. I made a big swing, hit a real peach...and the cannon didn't work! They asked me to do it again and this time, off a downhill lie in street shoes, the cannon certainly went off, the earth moved and not surprisingly I hit the ball like a damp squid into the water. I clowned about a little, to entertain the spectators, but one American reporter took great delight the following morning in suggesting that I made a mockery of the ceremony. Nothing could be further from the truth

It was at the Memorial Tournament in the United States in May of 1985 that I had my first full session with David Leadbetter. We had met at Sun City in 1984, and he had given me a few things to think about, and at the Memorial I said: 'Come on then, throw the book at me!' David did just that. He wanted me to work on a new backswing and change things that I had done throughout my golfing career. He told me it would feel weird and it did. But I had faith, which was an important factor at that time, in David and persevered.

David, who in fact was born in Woking, Surrey, had moved to Zimbabwe at the age of seven. There he played golf in his

formative years with the likes of Mark McNulty, Nick Price and Denis Watson. David actually played on the European Tour in 1976 and 1977, but for financial reasons he decided to take a club job at Staverton Park in Northamptonshire. He later moved on to Chicago and then to Florida and he kept in touch with Mark, Nick and Denis. They all became pupils of his and benefitted accordingly.

His reaction to my swing when he first really analysed it that summer of 1985 was simple. He said that aesthetically it was one of the most beautiful swings in the business, but that it would never win me an Open Championship. He said that the beauty camouflaged the ugly bits; that there were faults there that would not stand up to the kind of pressure that I would experience at, though we did not know it then, Muirfield. He said that it would be taking a gamble to dismantle my swing, but that he knew I was talented enough to do it.

David was hard on me. He stressed that I would have to accept that the remodelling process would take two years. I must be honest and admit that at first I did not feel like going through that kind of pain barrier. I left Muirfield Village, where the Memorial tournament was being played, thinking that I would take some of David's thoughts and dovetail them into my game. Yet I knew, deep-down, that I was ready for the challenge. I got

home and vowed to myself that I would follow David's instructions to the letter and that I would make it.

I wanted to learn all about the mechanics of the swing and I began to realize how bad my old swing was. I cringe now when I look at it. With the old backswing I took the club inside, and then my hands would go up rather than remain on the same plane. Consequently I got into the bad habit of having what is commonly known as a flying right elbow. David taught me to flatten

my left wrist position at the top of the backswing so that the right elbow tucked in much better. I started to achieve a better turn by remaining on the same plane.

That explains the basic fundamentals of what I took on. Of course there was much more to it than that. When I turned round to David in September 1985, and told him that I felt I was home and dry, he simply shook his head in disagreement. I had got the backswing right but, after years of

playing with the same swing, I was getting myself back into the old position and making the same downswing! It was back to the drawing board.

Yet I never at any time lost faith in what David was telling me. I would return, time and time again, to work with him. There were thousands of doubting Thomases who could not see the sense in what I was doing, but I think I provided the perfect answer for them in the Open Championship at Muirfield

Ryder Cup Glory
1985–6

The 1985 Ryder Cup at The Belfry: Bernhard Langer, my partner, unfortunately knocked it into the water here. I pleaded with him not to go for it but he wouldn't listen. We had to take a drop and I hit a nice chip over the water and onto the green. Bernhard, however, missed this putt and we went three down. I went to Tony Jacklin, the captain, after that and I dropped myself. I was under too much pressure. Tony had picked me for the team and now, as I was going through my swing change, I decided that it was best for the good of the team to give him the option to make changes.

I was determined that we should win, and I felt that the best way for me to work for Tony was from off the fairways. It had been a difficult year, and only I knew at the time how much working on my swing was taking out of me

There was a rare chance for me to celebrate that year when the Americans suffered their first defeat in the Ryder Cup since 1957. That week in September brought home to the international scene that the gap between the Americans and the rest of the world in pure ability terms had narrowed to virtually nothing

I began the match partnering Bernhard – seen here lining-up a putt with me searching for any hidden contours – against Tom Kite and Calvin Peete in the foursomes. I think Bernhard and I first played a competitive round together in the Greater Greensboro Open on the US Tour. That was at the start of the 1980s and he was 'yippy' even then on the greens. You try not to watch a player who has

that unfortunate affliction, but if you do then mentally you do not allow it to register. Yet I mention that only in order to stress again how determined Bernhard has been. You have to admire him for everything he has done. It takes a lot of will power to keep playing well from tee to green and not to get the score you deserve because you keep missing putts. And Bernhard is now recognized as a very good putter

96

Anyway we won the Ryder Cup and what a celebration there was for the team (left to right) that evening – top row: José Rivero, Bernhard Langer, Nick Faldo, Sam Torrance, Tony Jacklin (captain), Sandy Lyle, Paul Way, Severiano Ballesteros, Ken Brown. Bottom row: Howard Clark, Ian Woosnam, José-Maria Canizares, Manuel Pinero

I was happy with the way that I
played at the Dunhill Cup at St
Andrews – won by Australia –
because I had done six months'
work with David and for the first
time I was really beginning to get a
feel for the new swing

On Saturday 4 January 1986 at St Mary Magdalen's Church, Rodborough, Gloucestershire, Gill and I had a service of blessing, having been secretly married the day before at Stroud Registry Office. The dates were set apart so we could achieve what we wanted by getting married in private with just family and close friends – and no press! However, as predicted, they caught up with us on the next day outside the church.

It was a real white wedding in every sense. From leaving the church to arriving at the reception venue, a layer of snow fell

I had finished 1985 in 42nd place in the Order of Merit – my lowest ranking since I turned professional in 1976. It was a bitter pill to swallow. But I knew I was doing the right thing even if I continued to have some indifferent results in 1986. For there were now tangible signs that I was getting my new swing together. I finished 3rd in the Whyte and Mackay PGA Championship and 4th in the Peugeot French Open. I fancied my chances in the Open championship at Turnberry, especially as the weather was absolutely foul. I wasn't called the 'Rain King' for nothing, and I felt that I could turn my career around again that week in Scotland

David Leadbetter came to Turnberry, and he confirmed that the swing was in great shape, as do these pictures taken from different angles at the world-famous 9th tee. The trouble was Greg Norman was in outstanding form. His 63 on the second day was a remarkable round of golf, matching the championship record, and I knew that I would have to produce something special in the third round. It didn't happen because I took 76, but a last round of 70 still gave me 5th position

My third coach! After Ian Connelly and David Leadbetter comes Goofy. I was back at the Walt Disney World Golf Classic in Orlando. In 1983 I had gone there needing a good result to retain my playing privileges for the European Tour. I tied for second place and made it easily. Now I was in the same position. This time fortune did not smile on me. It ended a miserable year – apart from the Open – for me on the fairways but not off them as far as Gill and I were concerned

For on 18 September 1986 Gill had
presented me with a beautiful baby
girl, whom we christened Natalie
Lauren

103

On Course for the Open
1987–

Getting out of trouble at the 8th hole in the final round
of the Open

I made an inauspicious start to 1987. I went to Australia and I was awful. There is no other word to describe it. I had taken my first genuine break from the game – six weeks without touching a club – since turning professional. I felt that I deserved it, especially as it was our first winter at home with Natalie, and in total I had three months away from the tournament scene. I left Australia and moved on to Hong Kong and I played equally poorly there. I was concerned so I went to America to see David the week before the Bay Hill Classic.

David diagnosed why I had suddenly lost the touch for the new swing. What I had done during the winter was swing a very heavy club in order to remain fit. I had not only overdone it but it had made my arms tight and tense. David prepared an exercise programme for me which was designed to loosen up my arms, and I moved on to New Orleans where I played quite well. I returned home with my mind at ease again.

But I returned to America, first to play in the snow (!) in the Greater Greensboro Open – even they were suffering freak weather conditions – then in the Deposit Guaranty Golf Classic at Hattiesburg. It was difficult to go there because the tournament, although it carried official money, was played opposite the US Masters. I knew I should have been at Augusta. But equally I was determined that by 1988 that is where I would be.

Hattiesburg turned out to be a life-restorer to me. I shot level 67s and with four birdies at the last four holes I finished 2nd. It was an important result for my confidence. I went on to the Sea Pines Heritage Classic where I played well until the last day. Even so I returned to Europe, where I knew I would have to play for 1987, with a renewed zest. I was ready for the challenge

again. I returned to the old war grounds of the Madrid and Italian Open, where I had not been back for years, and I finished 4th and 3rd respectively. I knew it was

beginning to happen for me again. David had said it would take approximately two years. I felt certain his prediction was going to come true

It was on the Las Brisas course in southern Spain that it finally all came together again. Severiano Ballesteros's company was running the Peugeot Spanish Open and he had ordered them to make sure that the course was tough...very tough. That suited me. I wanted a true test for my new swing because I felt now that I was ready to win a tournament. On tough courses, when the greens are hard and fast, you have to accept that you will get good and bad breaks. It means that you will miss greens and so it is important to remain cool and composed. I played with Seve in the third round and I was in four bunkers on the back nine. But I managed to get the ball up and down in two on every occasion – always hitting it stiff as here at the 16th where the ball finished only six inches from the cup. In fact I was in eleven bunkers during that week, and I managed to get up and down all but once. A lot earlier in the year I had been unhappy with my bunker play. So I went into the loft at home and I got out all my sand wedges – approximately thirty – and I went into a bunker at Wentworth to practise. In the end I decided to keep my faithful Wilson 66 in the bag. I bought it three years earlier for $150 from a friend in Los Angeles called Mark Wildey, who is a classic club dealer. The irony of keeping that wedge in the bag was that I also signed a contract the week before the Spanish Open to play Wilson clubs!

Sometime the pins were put in places that were too difficult considering how hard and fast the greens were. Jack Nicklaus had jetted in that week because his son, Jack Jnr, was playing and he took one look at the course and said that the cream would rise to the top

I approach the last hole. I hit a
metal wood then a five iron to 30
feet. Coincidentally I would two
months later be using the same
clubs on the last hole to win another
108   prize. This time, however, I

carefully two-putted. I had won. I
had won after three years in the
shadows. A feeling of utter relief
passed through me. I turned to my
caddie, Andy Prodger, and I just
said: 'I've made it! I've made it!'

It was such a marvellous feeling to get my hands on a trophy again. It was my fourteenth victory as a professional – and so, for the superstitious, I had finally got off the number thirteen mark. We dined at Silks restaurant that evening and talked long into the early hours.

From left to right: Andy Prodger, Chris Dobson, Kevin Woodward, Roger Dobson, John Fitzpatrick, Sandra Fitzpatrick, NF and GF. Whoever doesn't smile pays the bill!

111

I continued the season with several solid performances, which included finishing joint 2nd in the Belgian Open when the last round was cancelled so giving me no chance to go for the title. David gave me a thorough check-up and pronounced: 'You're ready – now go and do it.'

My thirtieth birthday was on the Saturday of Open Championship week, but Gill gave me one of my presents early. She had the sweater custom-knitted, then decided that she liked it so much that she had one done for herself and one for Natalie. In fact I should have worn it on Saturday, when the weather was foul, but I think Pringle would have objected! We stayed in the Marine Hotel in North Berwick, and this picture was actually taken in the grounds there on the eve of the Open. Four nights later the champagne corks would be popping in a private room as we celebrated my victory

The trick with Muirfield is to adhere to a chosen game plan. The premium is placed on driving the ball into the correct position, as the fairways are ingeniously bunkered, and the choice of club – driver, three wood or one iron – is critical off the tee.

It is, of course, easier said than done. Yet I felt that over the first two days of the 116th Open Championship I came as close as one could hope to carrying out my own preconceived plans. My opening 68 provided a sound foundation on which to build, though the Australian Rodger Davis moved smartly into the lead with his 64, but I had more regard for my second round of 69. I was out early in the day and the persistent rain meant that it was all the more important to concentrate on steering a safe passage around the 6963 yards which make up Muirfield's par-71 Championship examination.

The plan, quite simply, was not to take any gambles. One wayward shot on a course such as Muirfield can, if you are unfortunate, lead to a penalty which is too severe for the 'crime' committed. Coincidentally Arnold Palmer admitted on the Friday at Muirfield to 'taking a gamble and paying for it'. He tried to force something out of the 14th hole after driving into a bunker, and he eventually walked off the green with a *ten* on his card. It had taken him five shots to escape from a greenside bunker. He had, at the age of fifty-seven, turned back the years to be in contention and then, after that 14th hole, he was out of the Championship.

Willing in a putt

I take shelter behind an umbrella on day three

I made mistakes at the 14th and 15th holes in the second round, but on each occasion it cost me only the one shot. Mostly I was happy with the way I swung my way around Muirfield's two splendid loops of nine holes. I hit a seven iron to four feet for a two at the 180 yards-4th. My five iron to three feet for another birdie at the 8th filled me with confidence.

I had brought over David Leadbetter from Florida the previous week in order to fine-tune

my swing during the Bell's Scottish Open at Gleneagles. We took a video of the swing and I kept that to turn to for confirmation after David had sorted out a couple of things for me.

Then a 69, for a halfway aggregate of 137, was sufficient at the end of the day to earn me a share of second place alongside the American Payne Stewart, who had an equal best-of-the-day 66, Australia's Gerry Taylor (68) and Davis, who faltered with a 73. The leader now was Paul

Azinger, who was seeking to emulate his American compatriots Ben Hogan (1953) and Tony Lema (1964) by winning the Open at the first attempt.

I was to partner Azinger on the third day, when we both scored 71s despite being buffeted by 25-mph gusts. It was a difficult day and Paul continued to defy logic, for he had never seen a links course before setting foot that week on the first tee at Muirfield. It must have seemed so incredibly foreign to

I just miss a birdie
chance early on
in the final round

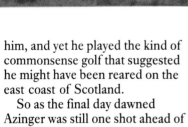

him, and yet he played the kind of
commonsense golf that suggested
he might have been reared on the
east coast of Scotland.

So as the final day dawned
Azinger was still one shot ahead of
David Frost of South Africa and
myself. One stroke further adrift
was the American trio of Craig
Stadler, with whom I was paired,
Payne Stewart and Tom Watson.
All three appeared to me to be
threats, but it was Azinger who
continued to bowl along in front.

115

He began the fourth and final round as if it were just a walk in the park. He holed a putt of fully 25 feet for a birdie at the 4th and another of ten feet at the 5th. He was out in 34. I could do nothing but make pars, although I was within inches of birdies at each of the first five holes, but I feel that it was the kind of round, looking back, of which Jack Nicklaus would have been proud. I recall Tom Watson once explaining how early in his career he had partnered Nicklaus in a US Tour event. Nicklaus did nothing spectacular. He simply played conservatively, because he felt that was the order of the day, and when he finished he had won the tournament.

Andy Prodger, my caddie, and I discuss club selection

On the 16th tee with Craig Stadler 117

I sink my last putt and victory is ten minutes away

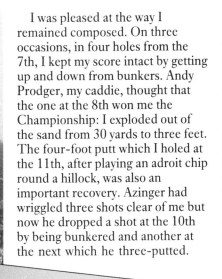

I was pleased at the way I remained composed. On three occasions, in four holes from the 7th, I kept my score intact by getting up and down from bunkers. Andy Prodger, my caddie, thought that the one at the 8th won me the Championship: I exploded out of the sand from 30 yards to three feet. The four-foot putt which I holed at the 11th, after playing an adroit chip round a hillock, was also an important recovery. Azinger had wriggled three shots clear of me but now he dropped a shot at the 10th by being bunkered and another at the next which he three-putted.

I knew now, as the mist began to clear and as I edged closer towards the clubhouse of the Honourable Company of Edinburgh Golfers, that I was within sight of the most elusive prize in the game. I stuck to my game plan when it mattered most, so that without taking a gamble I limited the risk of one destructive shot ruining what could be the most important day in my career. I parred my way through to the end and a 71 gave me a five under par aggregate of 279. It was enough to put Azinger, playing behind me, under pressure.

The scoreboard says it all

119

The speech I had dreamed of making

And the trophy I had dreamed of holding

We have all been in that position before. It can be so important to have your score on the board. Paul Azinger will have his day, of that I am sure, but on this occasion he was to meet his nemesis.

I had been nervous, of course, over the closing holes. I knew that during my last hour on the Muirfield course one mistake could ruin everything. Yet my lasting memory is of my five iron to the last green. I knew as I stood over that shot that it could make all the difference. I didn't want to sit back at the end of my career and accept that I had come close without actually winning the Open Championship. I knew that when that five iron shot – one which I had rehearsed on many occasions – deposited the ball on the green, I had done everything humanly possible to engrave my name alongside the greats of the game on the silver claret jug that is the Open Championship trophy

THE TIMES

First published 1785

Agony of silence for the victors and losers

By David Miller

Sport is characterized by a throaty roar of acclaim, at Twickenham, Aintree or Wembley, at an Olympic final or at Madison Square Garden. There is nothing to compare, however, with the massive, breath-held silence of 20,000 people at Muirfield awaiting yesterday's agonizing outcome at the final hole between Nick Faldo and Paul Azinger.

Sad, courageous Azinger. An almost funereal pall hung over the crowd as the luckless American arrived at the final green, bunkered to the left, to attempt to rescue a dream that had so wretchedly disintegrated over the two last disastrous holes. In a few moments his young, lean face perceptibly aged. Seldom have triumph and disaster been so unbearably held in the same palm.

Yet none should doubt that Faldo played a champion's round one stride ahead of his rival. With home expectation enormous, with his own ambition pumping, his nerve and his head still held steady. His sustained round of unbroken par contained moments of heroic calm without which the afternoon might have run away from him. It must be hoped that the champion's crown he deservedly now wears will enable him to be more relaxed off the course.

It is a reflection of the strained relationship between Faldo and the media that, with some 170 armbands available to walk the course with the players, fewer than a dozen yesterday followed the leading Briton, and this had extraordinarily diminished to four or five by the last six holes. It would be difficult to say whether that was an indication of disaffection or of the proclivity of the Press for working, at stroke-play events, from the tent.

Faldo must be praised for overcoming a few difficult years, on and off the course, for working diligently without immediate encouragement at modifying his swing with Dave Leadbetter, his coach, and for showing a champion's resolution when his chance came for the sweetest of success. To be popular is not essential to prizes. Let us hope this triumph gives breadth to his personality.

What was shown transparently yesterday was character under the stress of competition. Faldo came to the first tee with a previous best performance of fourth in 1982, fifth last year and seventh twice. Consistency would now be the key.

He was partnered by Craig Stadler, that portly American who must give his tailor a trying time. For him it was not to be a happy day. Starting at four under par, his challenge soon evaporated.

He has an endearing way of looking at departing, miscued shots like some lady with whom he has had an argument, half bitter, half nostalgic.

It was another day more suitable for fishing than golf. A grey sea mist rolled over the course, penetrating one's clothing, but thankfully the wind was nowhere near as fierce as it was on Saturday. Faldo's attack was quickly apparent.

Commendably straight off the tee, he was within inches of having birdies at the first five holes. As the surge of the sea drummed in his ears at the fifth, he heard that Azinger was now seven under, then eight under at the seventh.

If, unknowingly, the chance to have taken the title with more comfort had slipped away over those early holes, the core of eventual success came from the seventh to 11th. With a cross-wind at the seventh, Faldo put a five-iron into one of those fearsome bunkers to the left of the green, but escaped to within five feet of the pin. Bunkered again at the eighth to the right, he saved par again by dropping the ball dead for a single putt.

At the ninth he again missed a possible birdie, breaking off in hesitation when preparing a three and a half foot first putt: and missed. Bunkered at the 10th, he came out to within two feet.

Now, at the 11th, came perhaps the shot that won the trophy. His second left him close to the green but obstructed by a huge bunker with the hole hidden behind it on a slope running back towards him. He rolled his chip round the hillock to the left but the ball did not swing back far enough, and left him with four feet downhill requiring a surgeon's care. The ball dropped.

Now he knew that Azinger had shed two strokes of his lead and from the 13th to 17th Faldo gave nothing away as the mist turned to the finest rain. At the 17th you could barely see the grandstand from the tee. From 30 feet he putted to within 15 inches. With every shot the pressure was growing on Azinger behind him.

And so to the 18th, where Faldo fluffed his birdie, and Azinger met his nemesis.

FINAL SCORES

(Great Britain and Ireland unless stated)

279
£75,000
N FALDO, 68, 69, 71, 71

280
£49,500 each
R DAVIS (Aus) 64, 73, 74, 69
P AZINGER (US) 68, 68, 71, 73

281
£31,000 each
B CRENSHAW (US), 73, 68, 72, 68
P STEWART (US), 71, 66, 72, 72

282
£25,000
D FROST (SA), 70, 68, 70, 74

283
£22,000
T WATSON (US), 69, 69, 71, 74

284
£18,666.66 each
I WOOSNAM, 71, 69, 72, 72
N PRICE (SA), 68, 71, 72, 73
C STADLER (US), 69, 69, 71, 75

285

Faldo's dramatic win is worth the wait

By Mitchell Platts
Golf Correspondent

Nick Faldo won the 116th Open Championship at Muirfield yesterday to complete his emergence from three years in the wilderness of world golf.

On the day after his thirtieth birthday, Faldo put together 18 successive pars for a final round of 71, then waited as the luckless Paul Azinger dropped a shot at each of the last two holes and clutched defeat from the jaws of victory. Faldo's winning aggregate of 279, five shots under par, earned him £75,000 and the silver claret jug by one stroke from the Australian, Rodger Davis (69), and the American, Azinger (73).

Faldo said: "I knew I'd do

THE OPEN

25mph gusts that had buffeted the players on Saturday during the third round, after which Azinger led by one stroke from Faldo and David Fros' of South Africa.

The dream of glory di seven contenders, inc Frost, on the fir Murfield's two loops holes. Frost was be his putter and two along with Craig St Ray Floyd, so Fal moved along as threatened to pull c

Azinger had be by his friends 12 for staying at hom Florida, insist ing the Open. N thin man wh entally nces of istance us ri is so he e fro ar' n' c

Hunting Gate
HOMES
4444
LONDON AND MANCHESTER **25p**

Nick Faldo wins the Open by one stroke

By Michael Williams, Golf Correspondent

Nick Faldo yesterday became on sixth Briton since the war to wi Open golf championship when he bea Azinger, of the United States, and Davis, of Australia, by a stroke at Mu On a day of mist and high drama, Faldo, celebrated his 30th birthday on Saturday unprecedented — in recent times anyway for a 71 and a five-under-par aggregate of 2 He wins £75,000, though

SPORT
Monday, July 20, 1987

Sun
SPORT

GREAT NICK!

OPEN 87

Faldo pips Azinger by one stroke

BOTHAM'S TEST SNUB

By CHRIS LANDER

EXCLUSIVE

IAN BOTHAM last night refused to carry out England's order to prove he is fit to bowl in the Fourth Test.

Botham said: "I can't because of my septic elbow. Poison has got into my bloodstream."

Manager Mickey Stew art had demanded all-rounder Botham bowl a

long stint BEFORE re- porting to Edgbaston on Wednesday for the vital match against Pakistan, starting on Thursday.

Stewart alarmed that Botham hasn't bowled in first-class over for 23 days, flashed his instruc- tion to Muirfield where

Botham was watching the The Open.

Stewart said: "I want Botham to bowl and I don't care where it is — he can name the time and place."

But Botham, who missed Worcester's cur- rent game against the tourists because of a grazed elbow that turned septic last Friday, is

● Turn to Page 30

BOTHAM: "I'm not going to net practice."

THE DAILY TELEGRAPH,

SPORT 4

Faldo's steadiness is key to triumph

By Michael Williams at Muirfield

NICK FALDO yesterday became only the sixth Briton since the war to win the Open golf championship when he beat Paul Azinger, of the United States, and Rodger Davis, of Australia, by a stroke at Muirfield.

On a day of mist and high excitement, Faldo, who had celebrated his 30th birthday on Saturday, had an unprecedented, in recent times anyway, 18 pars for a 71 and a five-under-par aggregate of 279.

He wins a prize of £75,000, though according to his agent subsequent contracts should bring him a conservative £2 million over the next few years.

His voice choking with emotion, Faldo said it was "just wonderful," but he could not bear to watch as Azinger came to the last hole needing a birdie three to win and a par to tie.

The young American, 26, making his first appearance in

the players to hoot mournfully that they were approaching every green.

In this almost half-light, the championship came to its climax, Faldo striving tooth and nail for that elusive birdie, Azinger hanging on grimly behind him.

It was the American who cracked. While Faldo was escaping with a par-five down the 17th, Azinger behind him was about to drive into the 'Trevino bunker' from which he could only make short escape en route to a six and chip- ping in, as Trevino had done when he won here in 1972.

Faldo, of course knew none of this but he gathered himself for

Mounting pressure

Nevertheless Azinger had made all the running at first, a fine two at the fourth, a long pitch to the fifth for another, a dropped shot at the sixth, where another-bunker defeated him, but a long putt straight as die at the eighth.

Out in 34, Azinger seemed

Faldo, who wins a cheque for £75,000, will, in the long run, make a conservative £2 million mark stable, of which he is a client

He could never remember having had 18 pars before and that spoke volumes not only for the quality of his play but also for his resolution as frustration at the lack of birdies must have mounted.

Certainly there were some great saves, three times out of bunkers and one miraculously so at the eighth which, he thought, was the most crucial of all.

CARD OF THE COURSE

Hole	Yards	Par	Hole	Yards	Par
1	447	4	10	475	4
2	351	4	11	385	4

Faldo with w

's Nick Faldo celebrates his marvellous Open triumph at
s Claret Jug trophy

SPORTS GUARDIAN

David Davies reports from Muirfield on a dramatic British victory in the 116th Open

Faldo swings title at last

THE OPEN '87

DIFFERENT STROKES . . . Faldo holes decisively at the 18th; Azinger rues his miss on the same green

In surreal surroundings, with golfers materialising through swirling mists, Nick Faldo emerged as a truly substantial champion when he won the 116th Open, at Muirfield yesterday.

He became the second British champion in three years, following Sandy Lyle's win at Royal St George's in 1985, and he beat Paul Ainger with one of the most remarkable Championship rounds in Open history. He had 18 straight pars, a round of 71, and the only time he led was when Azinger missed a 30-foot putt on the final green.

It was, literally, a round *par excellence*, and it won for him the first prize of £75,000. His five-under-par total of 279 was one better than Azinger and Rodger Davis, who, with Ben Crenshaw, was the only one of the leaders to play a sub-par final round.

Better than that for Faldo, though, was the rebuttal of his critics, including this one, who have questioned the need for him to spend the better part of three years re-building his swing. His game has not, in fact, hanged that much, as he showed with some masterly scrambling yesterday. Bu the intense hard work he put into gain a full grasp of David Leadbetter's dictates, gave him the belief he needed to play his ...hen it really counted.

... many moments ... as

week. I had a good feeling all ...ek but I had to keep it to ...use you really look ...

to the 17th, had only a one-shot lead. At the 10th he had bunkered his second, at the 11th cut his drive into rough, but just when it looked as if he ... disintegrate he began to ... good shots, and ... to

ball to 15 feet but missed the putt.

Up ahead Faldo was playing a superbly judged 18th. A magnificent tee shot gave him a second shot that was between clubs, and it is an enormous tribute to his clarity of thinking that although it was four... he knew that ...ursing it

nervously and unconsciously hitching up his right sleeve with his left hand. His sweater, incidentally, had a pattern that resembled the blueprint for some complicated electronic circuitry and I daresay he would have welcomed a robot to take the putt for him.

But the moment eventually came when he had to hit it himself, and to an indrawn ... horror, he hit it five ... This was the ...

a par four on what Jack Nicklaus has called the most difficult finishing hole of any major championship course. It is 448 yards of bunker bestrewn terror and Azinger chose to hit an iron off the tee to take the fairway bunkers out of play. That bit was successful, but he now had more than 200 yards to go with his next, to a green guarded by sufficient sand to contain the entire championship field.

The American could not manage it. His ball trickled into the sand on the left and the huge crowd roared their approval. It is a moot point as to whether in these circumstances they were cheering the mistake or the advantage that accrued to the favourite, but it is an unfortunate fact of golfing life that it takes place.

Azinger had to stand partially outside the bunker to play his shot, and while he is the best in America at this department of the game, he could not hope to get this one close. Nor did he, and Faldo, barely able to watch the television in an R & A tent, must have known that only a fluke of Larry Mize/Bob Tway proportions could rob him of his first major championship. Azinger is also a good putter, but no-one is that good, and a few moments later Tony Jacklin's Ryder Cup team had another title to add to its honours list.

Faldo said afterwards: "I knew I may never get another chance and I told myself that at least I must try 100 per cent, otherwise I would not be able to forgive myself. I've had chances in the past and I didn't want to think, when the time came to hang up my hat, that I'd come close and not succeeded."

What does the Open mean to him? In material terms: "I'll get into every major for the next few year, and that's what we work for. And now I've done it once I can do it again."

But the story in the greenside tent was slightly difference. As he sat waiting for the award ceremony, he was overcome by emotion and had to be comforted by his wife, Jill. "You ...serve every bit of it," she ... worked so hard." ...

...DIAN

Monday July 20 1987 25p

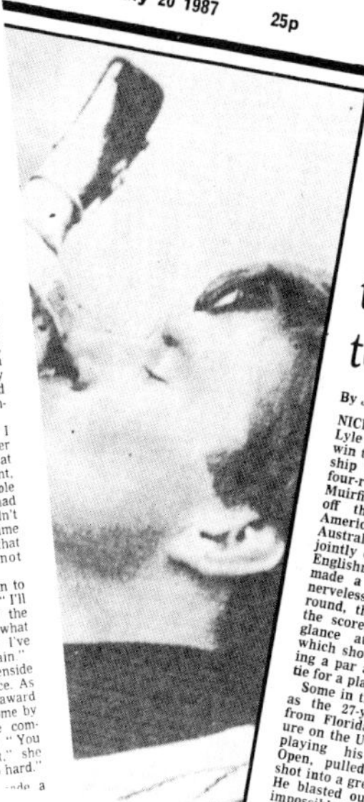

Ice-cool Faldo brings title back to Britain

By John Samuel

NICK FALDO followed Sandy Lyle as the second Briton to win the Open Golf championship in three years with a four-round total of 279 at Muirfield yesterday to beat off the challenge of the American Paul Azinger and Australian Rodger Davis, jointly one shot behind. The Englishman, 30 on Saturday, made a par 71 with solid nerveless gold on the last round, then marched off to the scorers' tent without a glance at the scoreboard, which showed Azinger needing a par at the last hole to tie for a play-off.

Some in the crowd cheered as the 27-year-old Azinger, from Florida, an early failure on the US tour, who was playing his first British Open, pulled his approach shot into a greenside bunker. He blasted out from a near impossible lie to 30 feet, but two putted to leave Fal...

Azinger blows up and Britain's leading hope at Muirfield claims his first major championship, an achievement which will make him a multi-millionaire

Faldo's celebration is par excellence

DAVID ASHDOWN

...g on the pressure to triumph in the Open

Tim Glover reports from Muirfield

NICK FALDO became Champion Golfer of the Year by winning the Open at Muirfield last night, the second British golfer to have done so in the last three years following Sandy Lyle's victory at Sandwich. Faldo received £75,000, the icing on the cake, and a splendid silver claret jug. It was simply par for the course.

Faldo, who was presented with a cake on Saturday night, to celebrate his 30th birthday, played almost faultless golf to go round in a pure par 71 and it represented another conservative victory.

He had 18 solid pars, no birdies, no bogeys, nothing flash and his first major championship triumph will make him a multi-millionaire.

Faldo had rounds of 68, 69, 71 and 71 for an aggregate of 279, five under par for the tournament and it was good enough to secure him a one-shot victory over Paul Azinger of America and Rodger Davis of Australia. "I knew I'd do it," said Faldo. "I knew I'd do it this week. Today, I was reminded of Birkdale in 1978, when I won my first professional tournament, the PGA Championship. It was misty then and it was misty today and I thought it was an omen."

Faldo rebuilt his swing, and his life, after winning a tournament in America in 1984 and he has had a lean time since. He became a pupil of David Leadbetter, a teaching professional from Florida, and the conversion took two years. "I wasn't happy and I had no direction," said Faldo. "I sought advice from David and it took me a hell of a long time to get things right."

The fact that Faldo won the greatest tournament in the world by par-ing every hole will dog Azinger forever. The 27-year-old American, who went into the final round with a one-stroke lead, had extended it to three by the turn, which he reached in 34, two under par, a figure which nobody bettered during the day. But Azinger, playing in his first Open and indeed his first tournament outside America, frankly blew it. He had bogey fives on the 10th and 11th and also bogeyed the 17th and 18th to come home in 39 for a 73.

Faldo was in the clubhouse at five under and Azinger needed only to make par over the closing holes to win the title. At the 10th he hit a two-iron, which did not give him sufficient distance off the tee. He failed to clear the fairway bunker and inevitably dropped a shot to go from eight under par to seven under. He admitted that he should have taken a one-iron. At the next, the 11th, he hit his drive way to the right and that cost him another stroke. At six under he was still in the lead, but at the 17th he hit a driver off the tee and later he said it was the shot that cost him the championship. He rolled into a fairway bunker, could only escape by scooping the ball sideways and the result was a bogey six.

"I made a couple of bad decisions on club selection," said Azinger. "What I did at the 17th was ridiculous. I should never have used the driver. Also, my putter let me down in the home straight. I had birdie chances at 12 and 14 and if I had taken either nobody would have caught me.

"But I don't want anybody to feel sorry for me. I have been five years on the American tour and this is the first time I've been in the hunt for a major championship. I am disappointed, but I proved that I can play with anybody in the world."

Even after his tactical error on the 17th, Azinger, the leading money-winner in America, only needed a par four at the last to force Faldo into a play-off. Azinger hit a good drive, but then hit a five-iron into the bunker guarding the left of the green.

As the ball bounced into the sand, the huge gallery encircling the 18th roared approval. It was a tasteless show of nationalism and it earned a rebuke from Alistair Low, chairman of the Championship Committee, at the prize-giving ceremony.

Over the last two years, Azinger has proved himself to be the best bunker player in the United States and in the third round on Saturday he found himself in a similar position. On that occasion he put the ball within inches of the hole, but yesterday he could not get it nearer than 30ft and he missed the putt.

Faldo had positioned himself between two television sets and refused to watch either. Indeed, thoughout his round he did not look at the leader board once.

Faldo had had plenty of birdie chances, although none were easy, and the key to his round was that he made several splendid saves. At the eighth, he pulled a three-wood into rough and played a superb bunker shot to three feet to save par. At the ninth, he pitched to six feet and made the putt after hitting a three-iron through the green and at the 10th he put the ball three feet from the hole from the bunker.

If luck plays a part in the winning of a major title, Faldo had it at the short 13th, when his tee shot flew left, caught the bank at just the right angle and bounced handsomely onto the green.

The 18th hole was no place for Faldo to change his par figures, but there was a concerted groan from the audience when his birdie putt from around 30ft was struck too solidly and the ball slid past on the right and stopped four and half feet from the hole. Faldo made no mistake with a stroke that ultimately won the 116th Championship.

"It may look like a conservative round," said Faldo, "but I was going for it 100 per cent. I played aggressively, but this is a tough course." Faldo, who was fifth in the Open won by Greg Norman at Turnberry last year, started the championship at 40-1. Norman made £10m from being the Open champion during the last 12 months, and if he never hits another golf ball Faldo can retire.

His affairs are handled by Mark McCormack's International Management Group, and in the press tent after his victory, Faldo spotted a couple of IMG representatives. "What are you doing in here?" he said. "Why aren't you out fixing up some deals?"

DAVID ASHDOWN

Azinger: Anguish as the prize slips from his grasp at the 18th ho...

After all the celebrations it was a fast drive from Muirfield to Edinburgh airport for a flight south so that I could be at Sunningdale to play in a special charity day for the PGA European Tour's own Benevolent Trust. There were pictures in the back garden with the trophy then, at last, I was able to relax at home with Gill and Natalie. But how the rich live! The first night we had fish and chips and the next evening a Chinese takeaway! We didn't mind. There was now time to be together and digest the full meaning of my Open Championship triumph

I went back to school the following Thursday... to Thumbswood school where twenty-five years earlier I had sat at this desk and learned to write my name for the first time. Mrs Mills, my first teacher, was there – though coincidentally it was her last day as she was retiring

From there I went on to play in a special charity match with Jerry Stevens, Frankie Vaughan and Hertfordshire amateur champion Peter Cherry at the Hatfield and London Country Club. I couldn't help doing my Frankie Vaughan 'swing' for my old mate Ron Marks, who put on the charity day, and for whom I had worked laying carpets in the winter of 1974-5

124

Gill's swing was modelled in Hawaii, where I gave her a lesson in 1985, then kept in cold storage until the 'birdies and babies' tour wives classic day prior to the Lawrence Batley International at Royal Birkdale. In truth my first duty as Open champion had been to give Gill another lesson, but when I mentioned how much it was for half-an-hour she said she would wait for Birkdale! We hit some shots the night before and we finished a creditable 4th in the event which was all in aid of a local children's home run by the Salvation Army. It was a lot of fun and at the 1st the other three guys all hit good drives and I drilled mine into a bunker. Gill was allowed to throw it out from there but she slipped and managed to snap-hook it into the rough!

Natalie will only know in years to come what winning the
Open Championship meant for Gill and me. But she was
there to share in the greatest day of our golfing lives

The sweetest of Ryder Cup wins and the European team (left to right) which made history by winning on American soil: back row: Seve Ballesteros, Gordon Brand Jnr, Sandy Lyle, Tony Jacklin, Nick Faldo, Sam Torrance, Eamonn Darcy. Front row: Jose Rivero, Jose-Maria Olazabal, Ken Brown, Ian Woosnam, Bernhard Langer, Howard Clark

My turn to play the captain's role in the Dunhill Cup at St Andrews, one week after the Ryder Cup, and Howard Clark, myself and Gordon J. Brand won it for England

Ian Woosnam, who finished 1987 as Europe's No. 1 money spinner, and I linked nicely to win 3½ points out of 4

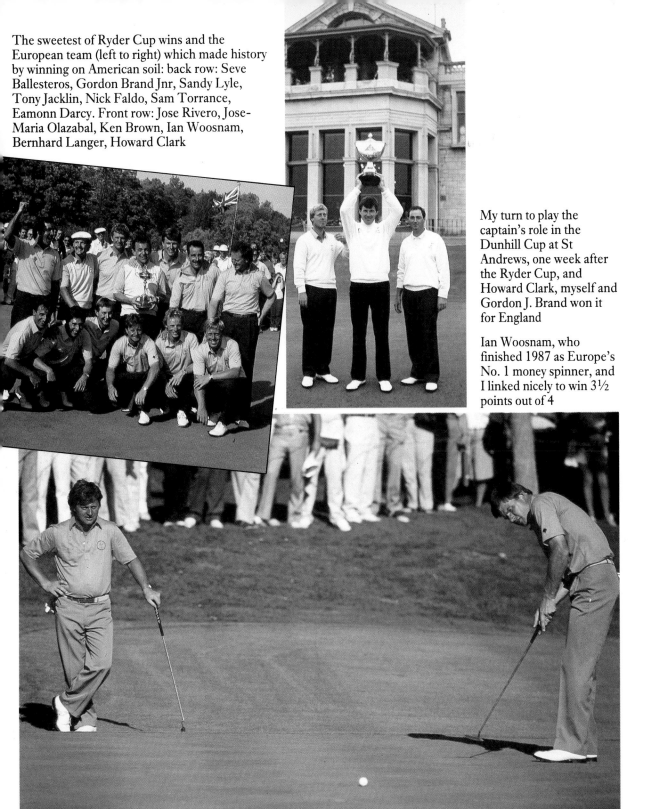

And a final word from
my sponsors . . .

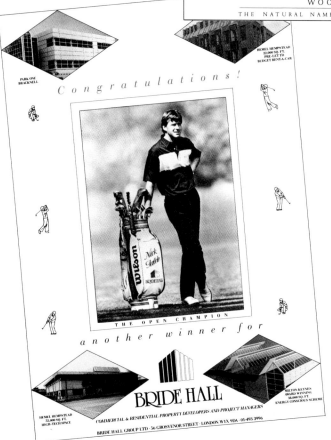